D1545001

EXTRATERRESTRIALS
CAN YOU FIND THEM IN THE UNIVERSE?

David Hawksett

PowerKiDS
press

New York

$$d = \sqrt{(x_2 - x_1) + (y_2 - y_1)^2}$$

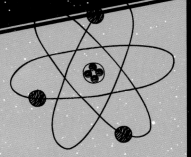

Published in 2018 by **The Rosen Publishing Group, Inc.**
29 East 21st Street, New York, NY 10010

Cataloging-in-Publication Data
Names: Hawksett, David.
Title: Extraterrestrials: can you find them in the universe? / David Hawksett.
Description: New York : PowerKids Press, 2018. | Series: Be a space scientist! | Includes index.
Identifiers: ISBN 9781538322949 (pbk.) | ISBN 9781538322017 (library bound) | ISBN 9781538322956 (6 pack)
Subjects: LCSH: Life on other planets--Juvenile literature. | Outer space--Exploration--Juvenile literature. |
    Extraterrestrial beings--Juvenile literature.
Classification: LCC QB54.H39 2018 | DDC 576.8'39--dc23

Produced for Rosen by Calcium
Editors for Calcium: Sarah Eason and Jennifer Sanderson
Designers for Calcium: Paul Myerscough and Jeni Child
Picture Researcher: Rachel Blount

Photo Credits: Cover: Shutterstock: EFKS center, Vadim Sadovski background; Inside: NASA: 19b, 32–33, 45cl, NASA/
JPL 26bl, NASA/JPL-Caltech 30–31; NOAA: UCSB, Univ. S. Carolina, NOAA, WHOI 24–25; Shutterstock: 3DMart 14–
15, 3Dstock 25t, 44cl, Paulo Afonso 38–39b, Carlos Amarillo 42–43, Catmando 12–13t, John A Davis 40–41, Elenarts
16–17, 27bl, 45tl, Everett Historical 18–19, GiroScience 11r, Jasmine K 34–35, Beat J Korner 22–23, Ksenvitaln 7br,
Liya Graphics 8–9, Erik Mandre 12–13b, Alex Mit 35b, Mopic 10–11, NASA Images 26cl, 27cl, Pixelparticle 26–27,
Plamuekwhan 14b, Targn Pleiades 21r, Albert Russ 9tr, 44tl, Ursatii 20–21, 44bl, Vixit 23t, Kishko Vladimir 9br, Marc
Ward 4–5, Bjoern Wylezich 6–7, Igor Zh. 1, 43t; Wikimedia Commons: Henrique Alvim Correa 17b, ESA/Hubble &
NASA 38–39, ESO/M. Kornmesser/N. Risinger (skysurvey.org) 37b, NASA 5r, NASA/JPL 41b, 45bl, NASA/JPL-Caltech/
University of Arizona 28–29t, NASA/JPL/USGS 27tl, NASA/Nova13 33r, NASA/Roel van der Hoorn (Van der Hoorn)
28r, Skyhawk92 36–37.

Manufactured in China
CPSIA Compliance Information: Batch BW18PK: For Further Information contact Rosen Publishing, New York, New York at 1-800-237-9932.

CONTENTS

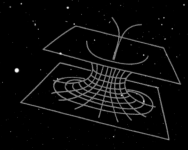

Chapter 1
ARE WE ALONE?

The ancient Greeks believed that Earth was the center of the universe, with the sun, moon, and planets all rotating around our planet. In the fourth century BC, the **philosopher** Aristotle (384 BC – 322 BC) wrote about the world as he saw it. He said there could be no other worlds or aliens. For centuries, this is what people believed.

Other Worlds?

Aristotle's writings may have very influential, but in 1277, the teaching of some of his work was banned. One of the newly banned ideas from Aristotle's work was that God was unable to create many worlds. All of a sudden, people were allowed to consider worlds other than our own, but most still thought that any God would probably not bother to create other worlds. Later, the philosophers Nicholas of Cusa (1401–1464) and Giordano Bruno (1548–1600) argued for the likelihood of other worlds. More importantly, they imagined them having life just like human beings, or perhaps even more intelligent.

$$d = \sqrt{(x_2 - x_1) + (y_2 - y_1)^2}$$

If advanced alien life exists, then it is outside the **solar system**. If any aliens ever visit us, they will be more technologically advanced than us. They will have to have technology that allows them to travel between the stars.

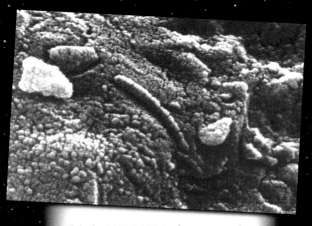

This is ALH 84001, the meteorite from Mars. In the center is a worm-like structure that scientists believed may have been a **fossil Martian microbe**.

Imagining Aliens

Fiction has always been ahead of science when it comes to alien life. The Syrian-Greek writer Lucian (AD 120–c.180) wrote *True History* in the second century. In it, people travel to the moon and are swept up into a war between the kings of the moon and the sun. It also has aliens, including dog-faced men. When H. G. Wells (1866–1946) wrote *The War of the Worlds* between 1895 and 1897, space exploration was 60 years away, and people were able to imagine aliens from Mars invading us. Now that **probes** have explored all the planets, we know there are no intelligent aliens in our solar system. But that has not stopped scientists from looking for more **primitive** life. When the US National Aeronautics and Space Administration (NASA) announced possible fossil microbes in a **meteorite** from Mars in 1996, the news shocked the world. Most scientists now discount this discovery, and it became yet another shattered dream of finding alien life.

WHAT IS LIFE?

If we are going to find life beyond Earth, we will need to know how to recognize it. Life is found everywhere on Earth, from the coldest to the hottest places, the highest peaks, and the deepest parts of the ocean. Life spans a massive range of forms, including microbes, fishes, birds, trees, and mammals like us.

A Common Definition?

There is no definition of "life" in general, but all life has things in common. It has complex **chemistry**. Life-forms respond to changes in the **environment** around them, like recoiling from something too hot or cold. They make copies of themselves through **reproduction**. They evolve, or change, over long periods of time as a result of **natural selection**. They use up **resources** to eat and drink so that they can grow, and they give out waste materials. They are made up of tiny bits called **cells**.

Carbon can take more than one form. Coal is almost pure carbon, and the graphite we use in pencils is made from carbon. Carbon can turn into diamond under extreme pressure and temperatures.

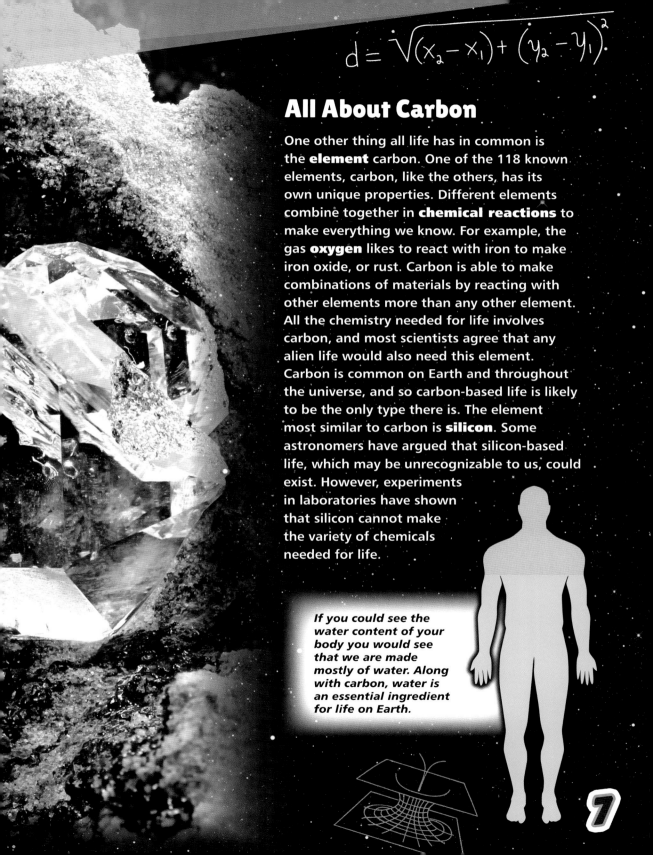

$$d = \sqrt{(x_2 - x_1)} + (y_2 - y_1)^2$$

All About Carbon

One other thing all life has in common is the **element** carbon. One of the 118 known elements, carbon, like the others, has its own unique properties. Different elements combine together in **chemical reactions** to make everything we know. For example, the gas **oxygen** likes to react with iron to make iron oxide, or rust. Carbon is able to make combinations of materials by reacting with other elements more than any other element. All the chemistry needed for life involves carbon, and most scientists agree that any alien life would also need this element. Carbon is common on Earth and throughout the universe, and so carbon-based life is likely to be the only type there is. The element most similar to carbon is **silicon**. Some astronomers have argued that silicon-based life, which may be unrecognizable to us, could exist. However, experiments in laboratories have shown that silicon cannot make the variety of chemicals needed for life.

If you could see the water content of your body you would see that we are made mostly of water. Along with carbon, water is an essential ingredient for life on Earth.

7

ALIVE OR DEAD?

Life is complex. Even the simplest life-forms on Earth have more complex chemistry going on inside them than all nonliving chemical reactions. Some life is hard to spot. Many sea creatures that live inside shells can look like rocks, and many of them anchor onto the same spot for life, like barnacles. If you poke a barnacle with a stick, you will see it quickly close up its shell as it senses danger. A tree is alive even though it never seems to "move." Its branches grow and it drops seeds.

$$d = \sqrt{(x_2 - x_1) + (y_2 - y_1)^2}$$

Contained within each cell in every living thing are coded instructions that determine what kind of plant or animal it is part of. We call this DNA. DNA is unique to each **species** and each individual plant or animal.

Be a Space Scientist!

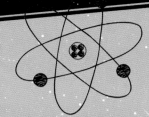

Are crystals and fires alive? Think about the properties of "life" on the previous two pages and the information below, and consider if the crystals or fire have these properties. Which two properties do they not have?

Crystals

If you dissolve salt into water and then let the water slowly **evaporate** into the air, the salt is left behind. It starts to **crystallize**. Tiny bits of solid salt start to appear, but instead of many small bits forming, the first small bits start to grow. They form a crystal with flat sides, making a cube. With our salty water experiment, you can change how the crystal grows by adding more water, or more salt. Just like a barnacle or a tree, the crystal has changed to suit its surroundings.

crystals

Fires

Like any living thing, fire can grow, eat, and give out waste in the form of ashes and **carbon dioxide**. Like animals, it needs oxygen to survive. Fire also moves as the flames change shape depending on their surroundings. We can see a fire respond to what is around it by pouring water or more **fuel** on it, and it recoils from wind. You can use a flame to light additional fires so, like life, fire can reproduce.

fire

Chapter 2
THE BEGINNING OF LIFE ON EARTH

Earth is around 4.54 billion years old. It formed alongside the sun and other planets from a vast disk of gas and dust. Grains of dust in this disk began sticking together until they grew into planets and moons. This process lasted 10 to 20 million years, until Earth reached its current size. The young Earth was very different from today's planet. For around 300 million years, **asteroids** and **comets** bombarded it, while it and the other planets sucked up smaller bodies. Earth's early **atmosphere** came from the gases and lava spewed out by volcanoes.

This artist's piece shows the early solar system. The young sun is surrounded by planets forming from the disk of gas and dust left over from the sun's creation.

A Quick Start!

Geologists have studied tiny structures in very ancient rocks and have been amazed at what they found. There is evidence that life began on Earth as long as 4.1 billion years ago. That is only a few hundred million years after the planet had formed. It seems life started on Earth just as soon as it was able to. While life was forming on Earth, the conditions on the surfaces of Venus and Mars were about the same as ours. It is quite possible that our planet was not the only one to develop life so quickly.

$$d = \sqrt{(x_2 - x_1) + (y_2 - y_1)^2}$$

Life Evolves

This extremely ancient life did not include dinosaurs or plant life. It consisted only of microbes. At the time, Earth's atmosphere was mostly carbon dioxide, with no oxygen at all. Somehow, though, the microbes began to photosynthesize. This is the process today by which plants use sunlight for energy and breathe in carbon dioxide and breathe out oxygen to live. The oxygen was the waste from the early microbes, and it changed our whole planet's atmosphere. All life on Earth was just microbes until 1.7 billion years ago, when creatures with more than one cell formed. However, it was not until 450 million years ago that the first plants appeared. The original microbes are responsible for the roughly 9 million species of plant and animal on Earth today. Those microbes are the common **ancestors** of everything.

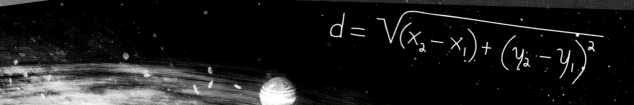

Single-celled life-forms, like these, were responsible for all the life that followed on Earth. Today, there are more different species of microbes than there are plants and animals put together.

COMMON ORIGINS

In 1886, the geologist Richard McConnell (1857–1942) discovered small fossils in the rocks at Mount Stephen in the Canadian Rockies. In 1910, US fossil expert Charles Walcott (1850–1927) dug a **quarry** in the area and gathered 65,000 fossils over time. Now known as the Burgess Shale, these rocks were 508 million years old and came from just after what is called the Cambrian Explosion.

An Explosion of Life

Before the Cambrian Explosion, life on Earth was simple. Most life-forms were microbes with just one cell, but starting 541 million years ago, and lasting perhaps 25 million years, a burst of evolution happened. All the main different types of today's creature came to be, and many of their fossils were found in the Burgess Shale. One of the oddest is known as opabinia. Like all the fossils in the shale beds, this creature was a sea dweller. Up to nearly 3 inches (7.6 cm) in length, it is known from fewer than 20 good fossils that have been found. It had five eyes on top of its head, with a soft body and fan-shaped tail. Its mouth was underneath its head and faced backward! Today, opabinia is **extinct** and no creatures on Earth resemble it.

$$d \doteq \sqrt{(x_2 - x_1) + (y_2 - y_1)^2}$$

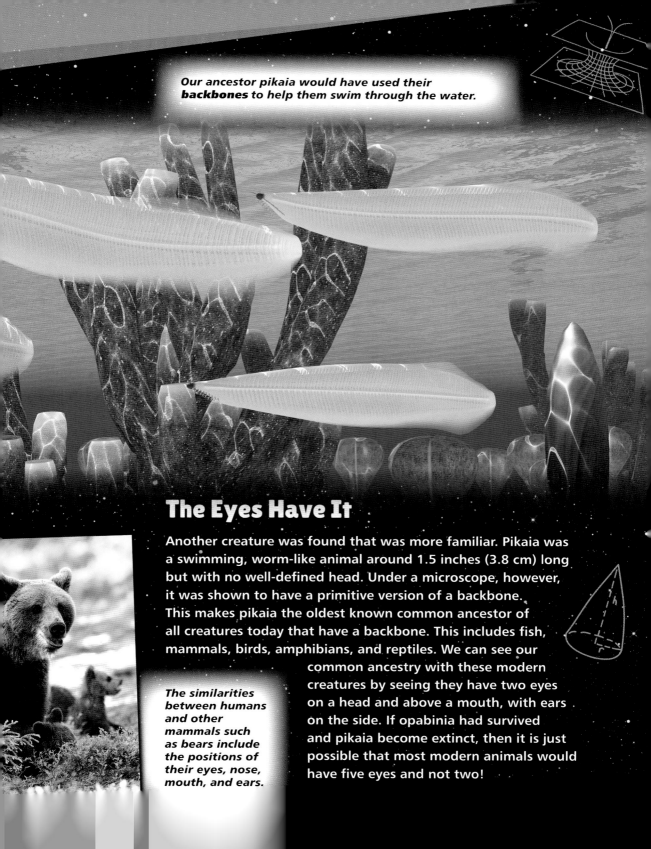

*Our ancestor pikaia would have used their **backbones** to help them swim through the water.*

The Eyes Have It

Another creature was found that was more familiar. Pikaia was a swimming, worm-like animal around 1.5 inches (3.8 cm) long but with no well-defined head. Under a microscope, however, it was shown to have a primitive version of a backbone. This makes pikaia the oldest known common ancestor of all creatures today that have a backbone. This includes fish, mammals, birds, amphibians, and reptiles. We can see our common ancestry with these modern creatures by seeing they have two eyes on a head and above a mouth, with ears on the side. If opabinia had survived and pikaia become extinct, then it is just possible that most modern animals would have five eyes and not two!

The similarities between humans and other mammals such as bears include the positions of their eyes, nose, mouth, and ears.

LITTLE GREEN MEN

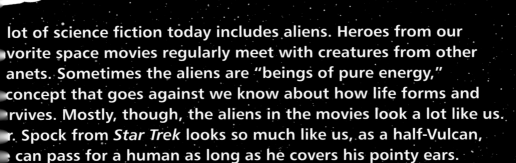

A lot of science fiction today includes aliens. Heroes from our favorite space movies regularly meet with creatures from other planets. Sometimes the aliens are "beings of pure energy," a concept that goes against we know about how life forms and survives. Mostly, though, the aliens in the movies look a lot like us. Mr. Spock from *Star Trek* looks so much like us, as a half-Vulcan, he can pass for a human as long as he covers his pointy ears. Chewbacca from *Star Wars* could be mistaken for a very tall human if he were wrapped in a cloak and hood. Many of our movie aliens have two legs, two arms, a body, and a head on the top. They even mostly have two eyes above a mouth, with a nose in the middle.

Science Fact

many movie aliens look human-shaped simply because it is much cheaper dress an actor in a costume and use makeup than it is to create a character that looks truly alien. However, true life on Earth is much more diverse than aliens we see in the movies. Can you think of any Earthling life that seems more alien than fictional characters? Pikaia may be the ancestor of backboned creatures but there are other types of life on Earth — spiders, trees, mushrooms, jellyfish, snails, and so on — that have no backbone.

Spiders look nothing like mammals. With their multiple eyes, they look more alien than most aliens in the movies!

$$d = \sqrt{(x_2 - x_1) + (y_2 - y_1)^2}$$

Be a Space Scientist!

The term "Little Green Men from Outer Space" is common when describing aliens in science fiction. Is it imaginative enough when you consider the huge range of life that might exist in space? What do you think is wrong with the term "Little Green Men"?

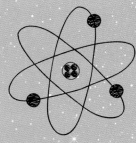

A typical Little Green Man from science fiction actually looks a lot like us. Often they are gray instead of green, but is this what aliens from other worlds would really look like?

Chapter 3
LIFE ON VENUS AND MARS

Could extraterrestrials live on the planets closest to Earth – Venus and Mars? Before the invention of modern scientific equipment, many people believed that they could. Today, powerful telescopes and space probes have allowed us to explore these planets. We now know that life almost certainly does not exist there.

What Lies Beneath?

Venus is the nearest planet to Earth. It is the same size as Earth, but is closer to the sun. Before the invention of space probes, astronomers could not see Venus's surface because it is hidden beneath thick clouds. Some astronomers believed that under the clouds was an Earthlike environment, rich in plant and animal life. They wondered if alien life-forms could exist there. However, in the early 1960s, data from space probes revealed Venus's surface. The data showed that the conditions there were extremely harsh. Life as we know it is not possible there.

*NASA's **Magellan** spacecraft spent four years **orbiting** Venus. Its onboard radar allowed it to see beneath the thick clouds and map the planet's surface.*

The Work of Martians

Mars is colder and smaller than Earth. It is slightly farther away from Earth than Venus. It has a thin atmosphere with few clouds, so its surface can be seen through any telescope. In the late nineteenth century, the Italian astronomer Giovanni Schiaparelli (1835–1910) studied the planet through his telescope. He believed that he saw long, dark lines crisscrossing the surface of Mars. People became very excited at this news, imagining that the lines might even be canals dug by Martians! However, we know today that the lines were just an **illusion**, probably caused by eyestrain from staring through a low-power telescope for many hours.

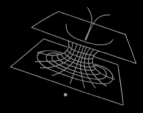

In 1898, H. G. Wells's book The War of the Worlds *was published. Wells imagined that a highly advanced species of Martians invaded Earth. In 1938, Orson Wells broadcast a radio adaptation of his novel* The War of the Worlds. *It sounded like a news broadcast and warned people that aliens had come to Earth! Many listeners believed what they were hearing and panicked.*

MOON GERMS

The Apollo Program is probably the biggest achievement in space exploration so far. Between 1968 and 1972, NASA sent nine manned missions to the moon, with six of them landing on its surface. The first to land was *Apollo 11* in July 1969. Mike Collins (b. 1930) remained orbiting the moon in the Command Module while Neil Armstrong (1930–2012) and Buzz Aldrin (b. 1930) descended to the surface in the **lander**.

$$d = \sqrt{(x_2 - x_1)^2 + (y_2 - y_1)^2}$$

Alien Outbreak

Just two months earlier, US author Michael Crichton had published the novel *The Andromeda Strain*. In this story, a **satellite** crashed to Earth, and the people in the nearest town were found dead. A meteorite carrying alien germs had hit the satellite, causing the crash. This allowed the alien germs to spread, killing everyone they touched. The idea of an extraterrestrial disease was terrifying for everyone.

This is a photograph of Earth rising over the surface of the moon, taken by the crew of Apollo 11. The moon's surface looks gray and lifeless compared with Earth's.

Exposed to Infection

Before *Apollo 11*, only robots had landed on the moon, and none had come back to Earth. *Apollo 11* was the first craft that took people to touch another world. They were definitely coming back, and there was no way to avoid exposing the crew to any potential moon germs. The fine lunar dust got everywhere. After each walk on the moon's surface, the astronauts' suits were covered in it.

When *Apollo 11* returned to Earth, the astronauts were put into **quarantine**. Scientists were more than 99% sure there were no moon germs, but the risk was still too high. Armstrong, Aldrin, and Collins spent three weeks in a converted trailer that filtered the air to keep any germs from escaping. The men were fine, but NASA continued to quarantine lunar landing crews until the end of the *Apollo 14* mission. Scientists finally concluded that the moon was lifeless, just as predicted.

On the moon there is no atmosphere and the sky is black even during the day. Here an astronaut sets up a science experiment with the lunar lander in the background.

UFOs

In 1440 BC, the Egyptian **pharaoh** Thutmose III reported seeing "fiery disks" in the sky. This was one of the earliest recordings of an Unidentified Flying Object (UFO) sighting. In 214 BC, the Roman historian Livy (64 or 59 BC–AD 17) recorded that "ships had shone forth from the sky." Since ancient times, reports of UFOs have been common. Often described as fiery, metallic, or round, these objects are sometimes believed to be visits from intelligent aliens.

Hoax Sightings

Photography began in the nineteenth century and by the twentieth century, its use was widespread. This changed the nature of UFO sightings as some witnesses were able to capture photographs of the so-called alien ships. Almost all have been proven to be fake. The "ship" in the sky was usually a small model held close to the camera.

Close Encounters

When Stephen Spielberg's movie *Close Encounters of the Third Kind* was released in 1977, reports of UFOs across US skies increased. Some people even claimed to have seen ships land before meeting the aliens, just like in the movie. An unfamiliar object in the sky can be hard to judge. It is impossible to tell how large or far away the object is, unless we know what it is. For example, if we see a bird shape, we know it is small and close by, but a plane shape is going to be something bigger and more distant. This is especially true at night, when our eyes do not function as well as in daylight.

$$d = \sqrt{(x_2 - x_1)^2 + (y_2 - y_1)^2}$$

Be a Space Scientist!

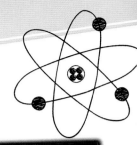

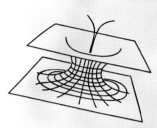

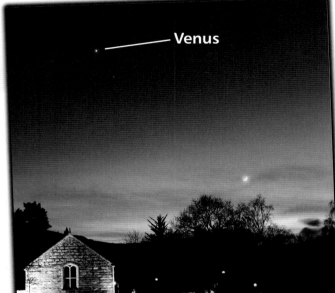

Venus

One rule used by scientists is that the simplest explanations are usually the best ones. Known as Occam's razor, this rule trims away the ridiculous explanations until all the simple ones remain to be considered and ruled out one by one. Many modern UFO witnesses have simply seen Venus sparkling in the night sky. What other natural or human-made things could be mistaken for alien ships?

In this illustration, an alien spaceship hides in the clouds. There is no evidence this has ever happened, but each year, thousands of people still claim to have seen UFOs. One of the most common shapes reported is a round disk, which has led to the nickname "flying saucers."

Chapter 4
FINDING EXTRATERRESTRIALS

Space exploration has proved to us that there are no highly advanced Martians or **Venusians**. However, we still have no real idea what alien life may look like. The biggest clue is the history of life on Earth. Remember that, before the Cambrian Explosion 541 million years ago, life was mainly microbes. So for most of Earth's history, germs ruled the planet. If we are going looking for alien life, then perhaps microbes would be the best place to start.

Water covers more of our planet's surface than land does. The oceans are where life on Earth began, and more than half of all species on Earth live there today.

All About the Water

We have seen that the element carbon is critical to life on Earth and almost certainly elsewhere. The other crucial ingredient is water. All life on Earth needs water. Humans are typically 50 to 65% water, and even microbes need water to form the insides of their cells. Water is common in the solar system, as most of the moons of the outer planets are made from it. However, most of the water in the solar system is frozen as ice. Only Earth has liquid water on its surface. Earth orbits the sun at just the right distance for water to exist in all three forms: it is liquid in the oceans and rivers, gas in the air as water vapor, and solid as ice. Earth is at the "triple point" of water because it can exist in these three forms.

High above sea level, such as at the tops of mountains, the air is colder than at sea level and the ice can build up and remain frozen, even in the summer.

Just Right

If Earth orbited closer to the sun, it would be hotter. This would boil away the oceans and thicken the atmosphere. The thicker atmosphere would trap more heat from the sun, making Earth even hotter. This is probably what happened to Venus billions of years ago. If Earth orbited farther from the sun, then all the water in the oceans would freeze and all life would cease. Luckily, Earth is neither too close nor too far from the sun. Its location is "just right," and we call this distance from the sun the Goldilocks zone.

$$d = \sqrt{(x_2 - x_1)^2 + (y_2 - y_1)^2}$$

EXTREMOPHILES

Extremophiles are a type of life on Earth that thrive in extreme conditions. In 1949, scientists discovered a region at the bottom of the Red Sea between Africa and Asia that had water with a temperature of 140 °F (60 °C). This was a result of volcanoes under the seabed, which spewed out **superheated** water.

Black Smokers

In 1977, a further discovery on the bottom of the Pacific Ocean shocked scientists. Scientists found vents in the seabed from which hot water mixed with chemicals gushes out. The hot water erupting from the seabed earned these vents the nickname "black smokers." Even though no sunlight reaches the Pacific Ocean floor and there is no oxygen present, the black smokers are teeming with life. Rather than just microbes, there are giant clams and creatures known as tube worms. The black smokers' microbes survive because they eat sulfur, a chemical in the hot water.

Hot water containing sulfur and other chemicals erupts from a black smoker on the ocean floor. Scientists use manned and unmanned submersible vehicles to study these strange features.

$$d = \sqrt{(x_2 - x_1) + (y_2 - y_1)^2}$$

The Water Bear

Elsewhere on Earth, the toughest creature is probably the tardigrade, or water bear. This microscopic eight-legged creature has been found from the tops of the highest mountains to the bottom of the oceans. Tardigrades can survive in temperatures from -458 °F to 300 °F (-272 °C to 149 °C)! They can even go without food or water for more than 30 years. They can survive **radiation** hundreds of times more powerful than the radiation that would kill a person and can even survive in the **vacuum** of space!

First discovered in 1773, the tardigrade is only around 0.02 inch (0.5 mm) long when fully grown. Tardigrades exist everywhere on Earth, from the poles to the equator.

Life Is Hardy

Microscopic extremophiles have been found living in the boiling waters of hot volcanic springs, deep within rocks in the Antarctic, and in water so acidic it would dissolve a person's flesh. Perhaps such creatures could have evolved on planets or moons under much harsher conditions than we could have imagined.

START LOOKING

$$d = \sqrt{(x_2 - x_1)^2 + (y_2 - y_1)^2}$$

Thanks to the Apollo missions to the moon, we know our nearest neighbor has no life. The moon has no air or water to support even the most basic microbes. However, now that we know how tough life on Earth can be, is it time to rethink where in the solar system we could find life, if it exists?

Consider the following information:

Mercury

Temperature	-275 °F to 840 °F (-171 °C to 449 °C)
Atmosphere	None
Water	Small amounts of ice in **craters** at its north pole
Gravity	0.378 of Earth's

Venus

Temperature	870 °F (466 °C)
Atmosphere	Around 90 times thicker than Earth's
Water	None on the surface, 0.002% in its atmosphere
Gravity	0.9 of Earth's

Mars

Temperature	-195°F to 70°F (-126°C to 21°C)
Atmosphere	Carbon dioxide, around a hundredth the thickness of Earth's
Water	Water ice at its poles, and ice underground in other places
Gravity	0.377 of Earth's

Jupiter

Temperature	-238°F (-150°C)
Atmosphere	Mostly hydrogen and helium, it has no solid surface to stand on
Water	Some water in its atmosphere
Gravity	2.36 times Earth's

Jupiter's moon Europa

Temperature	-369°F to -234°F (-223°C to -148°C)
Atmosphere	None
Water	Entire surface made of water ice and almost certainly an ocean hidden beneath
Gravity	0.134 of Earth's

Be a Space Scientist!

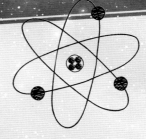

Look at the information here on some of the worlds in the solar system. Which places would be the best to find life? We know that life needs water, and since the discovery of extremophiles, we know life can survive a much greater range of conditions than we once thought. We also know that extremophiles have lived on our planet for most of its history. They evolved without oxygen around deep-sea volcanic vents. Do any of the other worlds in the solar system offer any of the right conditions for life to exist?

Chapter 5
EXTRATERRESTRIALS IN THE SOLAR SYSTEM

Humans have directly looked for life on only two other bodies in the solar system. The first was the moon, where Armstrong, Aldrin, and Collins tested to see if they contracted moon germs. The chances were very slim, but on Mars, the chances were taken much more seriously.

Mars Microbes?

When NASA sent the twin Viking landers to Mars in 1976, the search for life was one of the main goals. Each lander had an simple onboard chemistry laboratory. A robotic arm on the landers was used to scoop up soil from the Martian surface and drop it into the laboratory. Four separate experiments were performed on the soil samples. One of these involved feeding the soil a drop of water containing nutrients. The results showed carbon dioxide being released by the soil after being fed the water, indicating that something in the soil had "eaten" the nutrients. Unfortunately, the other experiments showed that this gas release was much more likely to be a result of chemical reactions, not life.

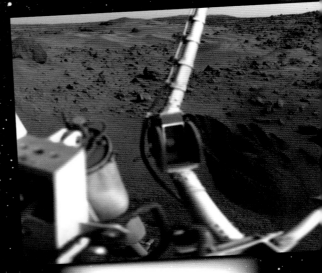

On the right of this Viking lander, you can see the robotic arm with the scoop at the end. On the ground in the center are a series of trenches dug by the scoop to obtain soil samples.

$$d = \sqrt{(x_2 - x_1) + (y_2 - y_1)^2}$$

The Same as Earth?

While the surface of Mars today is very hostile
to life, scientists believe that Mars and Earth had
similar conditions billions of years ago, at the time
when life began on Earth. This means life could
also could have evolved on Mars. If this were true,
then we have only had to travel one planet away
from Earth to find signs of more life. This would
hint that life would be widespread in the universe.

*Ius Chasma on Mars
is part of the huge
Valles Marineris,
the largest canyon
in the solar system.
It shows that there
might have been
a time in the past
when Mars was
warmer and wetter.*

The Search for Water

Today's Mars does have plenty of signs of water. The bright **polar caps** are
mostly water, and there are many surface features that could only have been
carved by running water. Much of Earth's atmosphere comes from volcanic
eruptions. The giant volcanoes on Mars have not erupted for millions of years,
but when they were active, it is possible Mars's atmosphere was much thicker
than it is today. This would have made it warmer and allowed seas and oceans

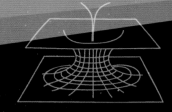

LIFE ON EUROPA

By the time the twin Voyager probes encountered Jupiter and two of its moons, Io and Europa, in 1979, none of the other planets explored had shown any signs of life. Nobody expected to find extraterrestrials on the moons.

Io and Europa

The Voyager mission discovered that Jupiter's moon, Io, was so squeezed by the gravity of Jupiter and Europa that huge amounts of heat were generated inside it. This heat causes massive volcanic eruptions on Io. Europa looked like a cracked eggshell, completely covered in ice. Europa too was being heated up inside by the same process as Io.

An Alien Ocean

When the *Galileo* spacecraft arrived at Jupiter in 1995, it entered orbit and studied the planet and its moons for nearly eight years. Its close-up pictures of Europa stunned mission scientists. There were hardly any impact craters at all. With no atmosphere to erode the craters, something else had to have erased them. Scientists believe that beneath Europa's icy **crust** is an ocean of salty water that wraps around the entire moon. The water is kept from freezing by the heat generated within the moon. At the bottom of Europa's ocean is a rocky surface where perhaps black smokers are erupting today, spewing out nutrients, such as sulfur.

$$d = \sqrt{(x_2 - x_1) + (y_2 - y_1)^2}$$

Exploring Alien Seas

Astronomers are desperate to return to Europa. If there is life under the ice, they will need a lander to find it. One possible future mission will land on the surface, drill through the ice, and release a robotic submarine into the ocean. If there is life on Europa, then this submarine will have to be the most **sterile** object ever launched into space from Earth. We would not want to risk giving "Earth germs" to the Europans!

This artwork shows a future probe returning to Europa. The disk at the top is a small lander that will search for life on this strange icy moon. Some scientists believe there is more chance of life on Europa than life on Mars.

DECONTAMINATION

$$d = \sqrt{(x_2 - x_1) + (y_2 - y_1)^2}$$

Throughout human history, diseases have been passed from one person to another. Sometimes explorers carried diseases and unknowingly infected entire populations. Imagine a space probe from Earth landing on Mars and contaminating it with microbes from Earth. It is possible that any Mars microbes would be completely wiped out by our own. In the search for life, humans could

Galileo looped around Jupiter many times, encountering its moons, including volcanic Io. Thrusters on the probe allowed fine tuning of its orbit. This allowed the probe to pass close enough to the moons to take detailed pictures.

Cooking Spacecraft

When NASA sent the Viking landers to Mars, it made sure there was no chance of contamination. Sterilizing spacecraft was first proposed back in 1958. The US National Academy of Sciences urged any missions to planets or moons to not pose a risk of contaminating them with Earth microbes. The 1967 Outer Space Treaty included this rule. The Viking landers were "cooked" for 30 hours at 257°F (125°C) to kill any Earth life before being sealed. Today, different methods of sterilization are used, including blasting probes with radiation before launch.

Be a Space Scientist!

As an **orbiter**, *Galileo* was not sterilized like the Viking landers. By the time the Galileo mission to Jupiter was coming to an end, *Galileo* was running low on fuel. Without fuel, *Galileo* would keep orbiting Jupiter and passing close to its moons for many years, but with no control over where it went. It could even crash into one of the moons. As a result, NASA made the decision to destroy the spacecraft. To do this, the spacecraft was aimed at Jupiter so that it burned up in the planet's atmosphere. The same fate happened to *Cassini*, when its mission orbiting Saturn ended in September 2017. Why do you think NASA made sure *Galileo* and *Cassini* were not left to orbit their planets? What might they have crashed into that could have led to contamination of possible life?

Cassini

Chapter 6
BEYOND THE SOLAR SYSTEM

In the solar system, Mars and Europa currently seem the best places to find life. However, there are other bodies that could have life. For example, Saturn's icy moon, Enceladus, is similar to Europa in many ways and also has an ocean of water beneath its ice. Pluto, first explored in 2015, looks like it may have a water ocean under its ice, so perhaps there is life there, too. But what about beyond our solar system?

Life in Our Galaxy

Our planet orbits a star, the sun, around halfway out from the center of our **galaxy**, the Milky Way. It is impossible to count the number of stars in the Milky Way, as many are hidden from view. However, as many as 400 billion stars are thought to exist in our galaxy. Many of these stars are completely unsuitable for life because they are variable stars. Variable stars swell and shrink in size and brightness. This means there is no chance for any Goldilocks zone to exist, and any orbiting planets would be alternately baked and frozen.

In clear, dark skies, a faint band of light can be seen stretching across the sky. Photography can reveal that this band is the combined light from millions of stars in our own galaxy.

Planets in the Universe

Most stars are not variable and shine at constant brightness, like our sun. Out of 400 billion stars, surely there must be a few more in our galaxy that can support life? Beyond our Milky Way galaxy are another 100 to 200 billion other galaxies, each with hundreds of billions of stars.

Having stars is not enough. There must be planets for life to evolve. Planets protect life from the harsh radiation and vacuum of space, and provide all the chemicals and nutrients life needs. It was not until 1992 that the first planet around another star was discovered. Two more have since been discovered in the same star system, and together they have been named Draugr, Poltergeist, and Phobetor.

Bright and dark clouds of gas and dust also make up this band, which is our own galaxy seen edge-on, from the solar system.

$$d = \sqrt{(x_2 - x_1) + (y_2 - y_1)^2}$$

EXOPLANETS

Exoplanets, also called extrasolar planets, are what we call planets orbiting stars other than our sun. Since the discovery of the first exoplanet in 1992, many more have been found. In March 2017, the grand total was 3,586 planets in 2,691 star systems.

Strange Worlds

Some of these exoplanets are very strange compared to our solar system. For example, Kepler-70b is a rocky world smaller than Earth that orbits very close to its parent star, so close that it races around its star and completes an orbit in just 5.67 hours! Compare this to Mercury, the closest planet to our sun, which takes 88 days to orbit the sun once. Kepler-70b is thought to be made almost completely of the metal iron. This means it was probably once a gas giant like Jupiter, but everything except its metal core was stripped away by the intense radiation from its star. This metal world is more than 12,000°F (6,649°C) at its surface, even hotter than the surface of our sun!

Kepler-70b bakes in the heat and radiation from its parent star. No scientists think that this planet is likely to have life.

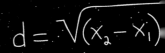
$$d = \sqrt{(x_2 - x_1)}$$

Other Worlds

Other worlds have also been spotted. In 2017, a system of seven planets was discovered orbiting a star named TRAPPIST-1. The planets all orbit quite close to one another and are all rocky worlds. Astronomers were especially excited because three of these worlds orbit within the star's Goldilocks zone, where liquid water could exist on the surface. TRAPPIST-1 is just 40 **light-years** from Earth and may be the best place to look for life outside our solar system.

If we ever travel to TRAPPIST-1, it may look like this. Three of its planets are seen here, all orbiting in regions where it is neither too hot nor too cold. When humans are able to build probes that can reach the stars, this system will be one of the first to be visited.

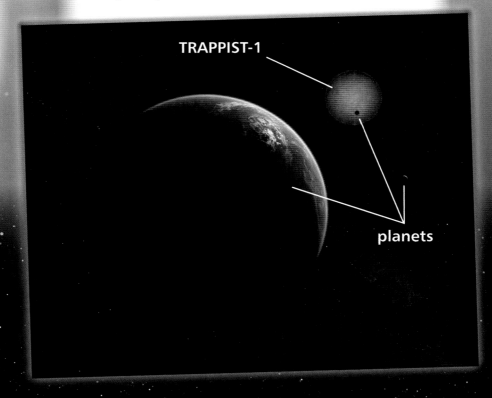

TRAPPIST-1

planets

HAVE EXTRATERRESTRIALS EVER VISITED US?

UFO sightings in ancient history and modern times seem to present evidence that aliens have visited us. However, none of these sightings have been proven true, and most are the result of optical illusions or mistaken identity. If any aliens have visited us, then they must have invented a way to travel between the stars.

Proxima Centauri dazzles in this image taken by the Hubble Space Telescope.

The Space Between the Stars

The nearest star to the sun, Proxima Centauri, was found to have a planet in 2016. Its distance, 4.25 light-years, means that a spacecraft would take 4.25 years to reach us, even traveling at the speed of light. Modern knowledge of science states that nothing can travel faster than light. TRAPPIST-1 is 40 light-years away, so a spacecraft at the speed of light would take 40 years to reach us. The huge distances between the stars makes interstellar travel difficult and unlikely.

$$d = \sqrt{(x_2 - x_1) + (y_2 - y_1)^2}$$

Wow!

These great distances do not mean that communication with aliens is impossible. Radio signals travel at the speed of light and, if aliens have been sending radio signals at us, we may be able to detect them. SETI stands for the Search for Extraterrestrial Intelligence. SETI uses giant **radio telescopes** to scan the skies for alien radio signals. In 1977, astronomers at the Big Ear radio telescope in Ohio received a signal from the **constellation** Sagittarius that lasted 72 seconds. The astronomer in charge of looking at results from the telescope was so impressed he wrote "Wow!" next to the radio signal. Today, this signal is known as the Wow signal. Forty years after this moment, there is still no explanation for the Wow signal. It has never been repeated but is the most likely candidate for alien communication that humans have ever received.

The Allen Telescope Array is a set of radio telescopes in California. It was built and funded by billionaire Paul Allen, who co-founded the software company Microsoft. The Allen Telescope Array is used to listen for radio signals from alien civilizations.

IS THERE ANYBODY THERE?

$$d = \sqrt{(x_2 - x_1) + (y_2 - y_1)}$$

One of the questions we have been trying to answer for decades is whether we are alone in the universe. Many scientists believe that given the incredible size of the universe and the sheer number of stars with planets orbiting them, we would be foolish to think that only Earth is home to living things. Mathematically, that makes no sense. However, proving it is another matter entirely.

Looking for Life

SETI has been carried out over the years by government agencies, universities, and private companies. One of the main methods of searching has been by analyzing radio waves from outside the solar system. Our own civilization emits a lot of radiation through things like television broadcasts.

Radio telescopes are used to communicate with space probes in the solar system. They are also used to study astronomical objects and listen for signals from space that may be artificial.

Space Signals

It is easy to tell if a signal is artificial or human-made. If we could find similar signals coming from space, it might be a sign of intelligent life. One new technique is using telescopes to search for alien laser signals. Lasers are a way of transmitting messages over huge distances, but the signals would be incredibly faint by the time they reached Earth.

Be a Space Scientist!

As a space scientist, it is your job to decide what is the most important information to send into space in the hope that intelligent life will find it. You should consider the following:
- What key data about Earth should you record? Why is this information important?
- How will you record the information? Consider the forms in which intelligent life might read it. What language/form of communication should you use?
- What is the best way to transport your data through space?

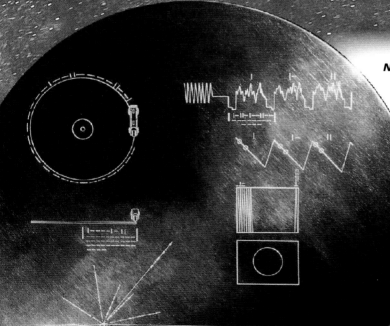

NASA recorded data about humans and Earth on golden records, shown here. They were sent into space on board both Voyager probes to tell intelligent life about our planet and the animals found on it.

WHAT IF THEY ARE OUT THERE?

The British astronomer and author Arthur C. Clarke (1917–2008) once wrote about aliens and said, "Two possibilities exist: either we are alone in the universe or we are not. Both are equally terrifying." You can imagine the fear of loneliness if we knew we were the only planet with life, but why would a universe teeming with life be so scary?

Colonization

The British physicist Stephen Hawking (b.1942) is also afraid of aliens. On the discovery of a potentially habitable exoplanet, he once stated that if we ever receive a signal from such a planet, we should be wary of answering it. Hawking was referring to our own human history. When explorers from one civilization met another civilization for the first time, it usually ended badly. For example, the Italian explorer Christopher Columbus (1451–1506) was arguably the man behind the colonization of the Americas by Europeans. The European soldiers slaughtered the people living in the Americas, stole their land and resources, and began trading human beings as slaves. Could aliens ever attempt to colonize Earth in a similar

There are three types of close encounters: when you see an alien ship in the sky, when you see it land, and when the aliens get out of their ship and meet people. This illustration shows the last.

$$d = \sqrt{(x_2 - x_1) + (y_2 - y_1)^2}$$

An alien civilization that could travel between the stars would be more advanced than us. They could even have technology that could hurt us, making Earth easy to conquer.

A More Advanced Species?

If aliens travel to Earth, then right away that makes them more advanced than us, as we cannot yet travel to the stars. If humans can treat each other so badly, then how would a species more advanced than us treat us?

Good Aliens or Bad?

Some scientists believe that visiting aliens would not harm us. They think that if aliens have survived long enough to develop **warp drive** or any way to travel faster than light, that would mean they have lived long enough to overcome their differences and avoid killing each other. Maybe they would be peaceful if they came to Earth. Radio and television signals from Earth have been leaking out into space since the early twentieth century. If they are close enough, then the extraterrestrials probably already know we are here!

8–9 Alive or Dead?

The crystal and the flame are not alive. They are not made of cells and they do not evolve.

14–15 Little Green Men

If life is common in the universe, who knows what form it might take? There is nothing wrong with thinking aliens may be little or green, but if they were indeed human-like with bodies like ours, that would be an incredible coincidence!

20–21 UFOs

If Venus can be mistaken for a UFO, then so can the other bright planets: Mars, Jupiter, and Saturn. With thousands of human-made satellites now orbiting Earth, they too are often mistaken for UFOs as they move across the sky in a matter of minutes. Flocks of geese at night, lit up from underneath by streetlamps, have been mistaken for entire fleets of alien warships coming to get us!

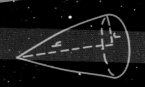

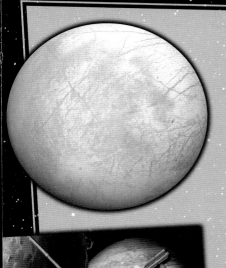

26–27 Start Looking

Mars and Europa are the only places where there is a lot of water, even if much of it is frozen. Mercury and Jupiter are considered highly unlikely places to find life. The surface of Venus is too hot for life, but it is possible that high in its clouds, the temperature may be low enough for something to survive.

32–33 Decontamination

Galileo and *Cassini* would have continued orbiting Jupiter and Saturn. However, these planets have many moons. By destroying the probes, NASA made certain that there was no chance of them crashing into the moons, which may have a chance of life.

40–41 Is Anybody Out There?

The golden records on the Voyager probes carry enough information for aliens to find us. Perhaps you could use similar records that include pictures of Earth and sounds of humans, animals, and nature. This would perhaps be easier to understand than a language. The sounds would also give the aliens clues to how we live on Earth. Until humans invent speedier spacecraft, sending information into space using radio telescopes or attaching it to probes are our best options

$$d = \sqrt{(x_2 - x_1) + (y_2 - y_1)^2}$$

GLOSSARY

ancestors An early type of plant or animal from which others have evolved.

asteroids Large rocks found in the solar system.

atmosphere Thin blanket of gas surrounding a planet.

backbone The column of small linked bones down the middle of a person or animal's back.

carbon dioxide A gas humans breathe out, which also occurs naturally.

cells The smallest parts of living things.

chemical reactions When two or more substances combine to form new substances, often giving off heat.

chemistry The study of what matter is made of and how it changes.

civilizations Complex societies of people who have developed communities, and culture, including writing or other types of communication.

colonization The act of going to live in a foreign place and taking control of it.

comets Chunks of rock and ice in space, similar to asteroids.

constellation A shape in the night sky formed by a pattern of stars.

craters Holes in the surface of a planet or moon caused by an asteroid or comet strike.

crust The solid surface of a planet or moon.

crystallize To turn into a crystal.

element The basic materials from which everything is made. Oxygen, iron, and gold are all elements.

environment The natural world in which plants and animals live.

evaporate When a liquid turns into a gas.

extinct When all the members of a single species have died out.

fiction Literature about imaginary people and events, rather than real people or events.

fossil Remains of plants and animals that died millions of years ago.

fuel A substance that reacts, usually by burning, to release a lot of heat, which can be used to power things.

galaxy A huge system of stars, dust, and gases held together by gravity.

geologists Scientists who study rocks and the surface and interior of Earth.

gravity The pull that any object has on any other. The bigger the object, or planet, the more gravity it has.

illusion When your eyes are tricked into seeing something that is not there.

lander A space probe that can land on a planet or moon and take measurements.

light-years Units of measurement for the distance light travels in one year. One light-year is around 6 trillion miles (9.65 trillion km).

Martian From Mars.

meteorite A rock from space that lands on the ground.

microbe A tiny life-form, including germs, which can be seen only with a microscope.

natural selection The process by which species of animals and plants that are best adapted to their environment survive and reproduce, while those that are less well adapted die out.

orbiter An unmanned spacecraft that flies in orbit around a planet for a long time collecting images and data.

orbiting Following a circular or oval path around an object in space as a result of the pull of the object's gravity.

oxygen A gas in Earth's atmosphere that living things need to breathe to survive.

pharaoh An Egyptian king.

philosopher A person who is a thinker and teacher.

polar caps Regions around a planet's north and south pole where ice has formed because of the low temperature.

primitive Of or relating to an early stage of evolutionary or historical development.

probes Unmanned spacecraft designed for exploration.

quarantine When something is kept isolated from others, just in case it has a disease.

quarry An area that is dug out from a piece of land or the side of a mountain to dig out stone or minerals.

radiation Energy in the form of waves or particles.

radio telescopes Instruments that receive radio waves from space and find the position of stars and other objects in space.

reproduction The process of producing young.

resources Things that people need or use, such as oil and fresh water.

satellite An object that orbits a larger object. It can be natural, like the moon, or human-made, like an orbiter.

silicon An element that is found in sand and in minerals such as quartz and granite.

solar system The sun, its planets and moons, asteroids, and comets.

species A group of similar living things that can breed with one another to produce young.

sterile Free from bacteria or other living microorganisms; totally clean.

superheated Heated to a temperature that is higher than its boiling point without being allowed to boil.

vacuum Place where there is no air, such as in space.

Venusians Beings from Venus.

warp drive A type of engine that is used in science fiction, such as *Star Trek*, to travel in space faster than light.

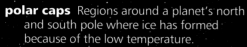

FURTHER READING

BOOKS

Aguilar, David A. *Alien Worlds: Your Guide to Extraterrestrial Life*. Washington D.C.: National Geographic Kids, 2013.

Aldrin, Buzz. *Welcome to Mars*. Washington, D.C.: National Geographic Kids, 2015.

Kenney, Karen. *Mysterious UFOs and Aliens* (Searchlight Books Fear Fest). Minneapolis, MN: Lerner Classroom, 2017.

WEBSITES

Due to the changing nature of Internet links, PowerKids Press has developed an online list of websites related to the subject of this book. This site is updated regularly.
Please use this link to access the list: **www.powerkidslinks.com/bass/extraterrestrials**

INDEX

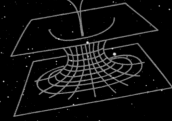